PEACE

TRANQUILLITY

AMRUTHA PHALA VALLI

I DEDICATE THIS BOOK TO ALL MY FRIENDS , PARENTS AND MY CHILD

Contents

Preface

- *This booklet, The philosophy of service, an approach to human development in India our attention*
- *and problems of our working class, comprises two illuminating talks by SRI SRI RAVISHANKAR GURUJI.*
- *It draws our attention to the subject of man and the problem of inter human relationship.*

Acknowledgements

- *When writing this book , I sometimes drew on transcripts of talks by what he said. Iam greatful to the Art of Living Foundation for giving me permission to this material*

Prologue

It is a small introduction of the material provided. It gives the steps to obtain peaceful state in this vast busy location.

CHAPTER ONE

<u>PEACE</u>

Pure peace of mind is something you can cultivate for yourself. It comes from getting curious about your thoughts and emotions, intimately knowing yourself and doing the inner work to shift your perceptive and relationship patterns.

How often are your thoughts running on the hamster wheel inside your mind? Worrying about aspects of your relationship, fearing things will never change or ruminating over what was or is happening? Not things that dull your mind into peace so how do you call a cease fire of the thoughts your mind is thinking, when sexual or relationship problems are plaguing you.

Curiosity is the most important quality you can develop to change a relationship pattern and peace of mind. Old patterns of frustration disappointment, hurt, resentment, guilt, blame judgment or doubt and experience, the flow of love that brings peace.

Peace is the path we take for bringing growth and prosperity to society. If we do not have peace and harmony, achieve political strength, economic stability.

and cultural growth will be impossible.

Movement, before we transmit the notion of peace to other, it is vital for us to possess peace within. It is not a certain individuals responsibility but to maintain peace but

everyone's duty
History has been the proof of the thousands of wars which have been taken place in all periods of different levels between nations. Thus we learned that peace played an important role in ending this war or even preventing some of them.

In fact if you take a look at all religious scriptures and ceremonies, you will realize that all of them, teach peace. They mostly advocate elementary war and maintaining harmony. In others words all of them hold out a sacred commitment to peace.

It is after thousands of destructive wars that the human realized the importance of peace. Earth needs peace in order to survive.

This applies to every angle including wars, pollution, natural, disaster and more.

When peace and harmony are maintained, things will run smoothly without any delay. Moreover, it can be savior for many who do not wish to engage in any disruptive activities or more. Moreover speech is personal which helps us achieve security and tranquility and avoid anxiety and chaos to make our life better.

HOW TO MAINTAIN PEACE
There are many ways in which we can maintain peace in different levels. To begin with human it is essential to maintain equality, security and tranquility and justice to maintain the political order of any nation.

Further, we must promote the advancement of technology and science w spread harmony. We must also recognize diversity and integration for expressing emotion to enhance our friendship with everyone from different culture mission.

Finally it must be everyone's noble mission to promote peace by expressing its contribution to the long lasting well-being factors of everyone's lives. Thus we must all try level best to maintain peace and harmony.

CONCLUSION

To sum it up, peace is essential to control the evils which damage our society. It is obvious that will keep facing crisis on many levels but we can manage them better with the help of peace. Moreover, peace is vital for human kind to survive and strive for better future, one of the healthiest emotions is anger. It destroys our ability to think clearly, properly and totality. Anger has also adverse impact on health. If you ask a selection of people what triggers their anger you would get a wide range of answers. However whatever the cause, even a single word spoken in anger can leave a lasting impression on a person's heart and has the ability to ruin the sweetness of any relationship.

A sage said, "How can there be peace on earth if the hich will ultimately benefit all of us. Humankind and maintain the welfare of people. In addition introducing a global economic system will help eliminate divergence, mistrust and regional imbalance.

It is also essential to encourage ethics that promote ecological prosperity and incorporate solutions to resolve the environmental crisis. This will in turn share success and fulfil the responsible of individual to end historical prejudice. Similarly we must also adapt a mental and spiritual ideology that embodies a helpful attitude to spread harmony. We must also recognize diversity and

So how can we set about creating that sense of peace within ourselves? It stars with the realization that we do have the choice to think and feel the way we want to. If we look at what it is that makes us angry, we might discover there is nothing that has the power to make us feel this way. We can allow only something to trigger our anger, the anger is the way in which we respond to an event or person. But because we are so used to reacting on impulsive, we forget to choose how we want to feel and end up reacting in appropriately, leaving ourselves with angry feelings

Meditation helps us create personal space within ourselves so that we have the chance to look, weigh the situation and respond accordingly remaining in state of self-control. When we are angry, we have no self-control. . At that moment we are in a state of internal choice and anger can be very destructive force.

Stability that comes from practice of meditation can create a firm foundation, a kind of positive stubbornness, others can whatever they want, and it may also be true, but we don't lose our peace or happiness on account on account of that. This is to respect what is eternal within each of us.

We give ourselves the opportunity to maintain our own peace of mind, because let's face it, no one is going to turn up at our door with a box full of peace and say, "Here I think you could do with some of this today!" there is method which could be described as sublimation, or changing of form with daily practice and application of spiritual principles in our practical life.

QUESTIONS AND ANSWERS

1. Do you think that a change towards a peaceful world, needs a change in the way people think? Can mind promote peace and is it enough to focus only on the human mind?

A thought process of persons require a positive attitude to promote peace because mind controls the way of thinking and behavior of human beings.
Mind promotes peace but a wrong mind or attitude can create war. Gautama Buddha also stated that all wrong doing arises because of mind. If mind is transformed then wrong doing remain?
The UNICEF also observed since wars begin in the mind of humans, it is also in the mind of man to make an approach in a peaceful manner.
To facilitate such an endeavor various spiritual principles like compassion practices like meditation perform peaceful approaches
Though violence does not originate only in individual but deep rooted also in certain social structures. Peace is a process involving and active pursuit of the moral and material resources needed to establish human welfare
2. A state must protect the lives and rights of its citizens. However, at times its own actions are a source of violence against some of its citizens.
Communicate with the help of some examples.

A.   Human beings created state for ones own protection of honors and property.

State maintain law and order. State maintains law and order. State protects the rights of its citizens by providing them a constitution, laws, police, judiciary and armed forces.
State make efforts to end type of violence created by social injustice and in equality
based discrimination like untouchability.

A state should avoid those actions which may be a source of violence against some particular groups.

3. Peace can be best realized when there is freedom, equality and justice. Do you agree?

Yes, I agree with the statement because; peace has occupied a central place in the original teachings of religions which has been advocated by various philosophers like Mahatma Gandhi etc.

Peace is an essential ingredient to establish democracy with two basic principles freedom and equality and justice and human rights.

Social inequalities and long practices of the caste religion, language may produce large scale evil consequences.

Sometimes, traditional system treats some people "Untouchables" and "peace" is meaningless for these people.

Discrimination against woman; women also given birth to female feticides, inadequate nourishment and education to grid child, child marriage, dowry, sexual harassment at the workplace, rape and honor killing.

The labor class which face the conditions to be paid low wages and ill-working condition also no meaning for peace.

4. Use of violence does not achieve just ends in the long run. What do you think about this statement?

A. Sometimes violence is justified to be used as liberation struggles to bring peace. But one violence is resorted, it tends to spin out of control, leaving behind a trial of death and destruction.

The pacifist advocate mobilization of love and truth to win the hearts and non-violence to be the methods of weak which has been rejected by Mahatma Gandhi who articulated different philosophy of non-violence. Nonviolence does not refer just referring from causing physical harm, mental harm or loss of livelihood and it also meant giving up even thought of harming someone.

5. Differentiate between the major approaches discussed in the chapter the establishment of peace in the world.

A. The first approach: It accords centrally to states respects their sovereignty and treats competition among them as a fact of life.

Its chief concern is with the proper management of this competition and with contentment and with the contentment of possible conflict through inter-state arrangement like "balance of power"

Such a balance is said to have prevailed in the country when the major European countries, their struggle for power by forming alliances that defer potential aggressors and checked the outbreak of a great war.

The second approach: It grants the deep rooted nature of interstate rivalry with positive presence

* 9 7 9 8 8 8 9 2 5 0 8 0 7 *